The Indian Boundary

Fireside Companion

History, Camping Tips, Ghosts and Mysteries

from the Cherokee National Forest

Joe Guy

Cover photo by Dan Frye.

ISBN:
9781793142221-13:

DEDICATION

For my parents, Danny and Rita,
who taught me how to be a father,
love the outdoors, build a fire, hunt, fish,
camp, cook over a campfire, and
appreciate God's creation.

CONTENTS

ACKNOWLEDGMENTS

Several folks are to be thanked for contributing to this book. USFS Archeologist Quentin Bass for providing maps and information about the area. Past campground volunteer Bob Miller, along with former Campground Host Genis Best and Retired District Rangers Wallace Graham and Steve Rickerson for their personal memories and experiences at Indian Boundary.

A special thanks is due to my parents for first taking my brother and me to Indian Boundary, where we spent our childhood summer vacations.

And to my wife, Stephanie. She took many great hikes with me to get the photos for this book, and provided much needed editorial advice.

Like everything else, I could not have done this without her.

INTRODUCTION

For over 40 years, I like many people, have camped, fished, hiked, or just spent a day swimming at Indian Boundary Recreation Area near Tellico Plains, TN. Visitors from all over America visit this recreation area tucked into the Cherokee National Forest. But it is also a popular destination for those of us who live in this region. Only 25 miles from our home in nearby McMinn County, this is where my parents took my brother and me on summer vacations throughout our childhood, and where my mother's family went camping when she was a teenager. It would be my senior year of high school before I ever saw an ocean coastline: my only beach was the Indian Boundary swimming area, and it was all I needed. I can remember riding up Highway 162, now the Cherohala Skyway, then called the Robbinsville Road, with my parents to meet grandparents and cousins on huge family camping trips here. Later, I would come camping with my buddies, and also took more than a few girlfriends swimming in the bright lake waters. Now, I bring my own family to enjoy the lake and the mountains. To this day, my memories are rich with the many times I have spent at Indian Boundary.

The evenings at Indian Boundary I remember distinctly. After the camp supper dishes are washed and the swimsuits are hung to dry, there in the whispering light and the warm popping of the campfire, stories begin to be told. At first, they will be the standard old campfire tales long told by generations of campers. But around some campfires, where the old campers recline in well-worn folding chairs, other stories are told by a few folks who know a little more about the darker secrets of Indian Boundary, and the Tellico area of the Cherokee National Forest.

I am, at heart, a storyteller and a local historian. Over the years, I have been asked to spin a tale or a ghost story or two around the fire. And I suspect that many others have found themselves in the same predicament. But telling stories about Indian Boundary is just not that easy. Most things can be found on the internet, right? Try searching for the history of Indian Boundary online: few results can be found.....strange for a publicly-funded project in a publicly-owned national forest. When doing research for this book, I was turned away more than once from Forest Service offices, and few of my calls were ever returned. Fewer still were my requests for records answered. It would seem that few records even exist about the building of the lake and the campground. Also, few are any real historical records about events that have occurred here, so outside of some general newspaper stories, there's not much else. It is, in a word, weird. It's as if some folks either have forgotten, or just don't want some things told. Indian Boundary doesn't always want to give up its history, or its legends.

It takes a lot of digging to find some stories, and the people who know about them.

Some of these stories come from area history, and these I have tried to give a few sources of reference. Others have come verbally, from the old folks who either live in the mountains or are life-long campers. All of the stories try to account for things like strange things seen in the campgrounds at night, or unexplained noises that have often permeated the dark woods. Sometimes it's footsteps in the leaves and pine needles, or eerie screams and moans that emanate from the dark woods....or the lake.

Ah, yes, the lake. Many stories seem to center around the lake. Some connect unexplainable things seen on, and in, the water. Others to a misplaced family forced to leave their home when the government made their property part of the national forest. Many stories are told around the campsites, but are they at all connected?

So sit back, gather round the fire, and read on. I've even added a blank section in the back so you can add your own memories of this great place. Maybe you will have your own story to tell of something mysterious and strange about Indian Boundary.

That is the purpose of this book: to help campers be more familiar with Indian Boundary and the area of the National Forest, enjoy some stories around the campfire, maybe take a few side trips, as well as to provide some additional fireside companionship.

On dark, eerie nights deep in the forest, companionship is a good thing to have.

The Indian Boundary "To Do" List:

___ Take a picnic in a picnic area or on the lake trail

___ Sit around a popping campfire

___ Walk around the camping loop roads and check out other campsites

___ Make a new friend

___ Roast a marshmallow, hot dog, or make s'mores

___ Go see the dam

___ Go relax on the beach

___ Walk, run, or bike around the lake trail

___ Fish from a pier or a quiet spot on the bank

___ Take a picture of the lake at sunset

___ Go swimming

___ Read a book in the cool of the evening

___ Sit beside a clear stream and listen to the bubbling water

___ Go out on the lake in a canoe or kayak

___ Cook a meal over a campfire

___ Lounge in a hammock

___ Shop at the Campground store. Get an ice cream.

___ Sleep in a tent, camper, or if you are brave....out in the open air

___ Tell or listen to a ghost story around the campfire at night

___ Play a guitar, or sing along, around the fire

___ Make a good memory

___ Play cards or a board game

___ Buy this book!

INDIAN BOUNDARY: A BRIEF HISTORY

Indian Boundary is a 96-acre lake and recreation area located 15 miles from Tellico Plains, Tennessee, off the Cherohala Skyway. It is known for its scenery, camping, fishing, picnicking and boating. The lake features a sandy swim beach, boat launch and accessible fishing pier. Its 3.6-mile lakeshore trail, along with its camping loops, provide for excellent walking and bicycling. For 50 years, Indian Boundary has provided a warm place for wonderful memories to be made. It is known as the "crown jewel" of the Cherokee National Forest.

Indian Boundary Recreation Area was built in the early 1960's as a project of the United States Forest Service with input from the Army Corps of Engineers. An area of wooded meadows called Whiteoak Flats, well-fed with several clear-flowing streams, was chosen near the base of Flatts Mountain to build a camping area, and later, a lake. A sizeable community had once existed at Whiteoak Flats, with several houses and farms around the present lake and some within its waters. A school once stood on a site that is now the southeast side of the lake, near where for many years the lake trail passed three giant oaks. Another home stood about where the current swimming area bath house stands.

According to long-time campground volunteer Genis Best, the man who lived there was reputed to be a moonshiner, who kept his gold buried in mason jars, although none have ever been found.

Around 1960, the Forestry Service bought up the farm land and tore down all the houses. Three camping loops, A, B, and C, (and later the back loop of C was designated as D) were built, complete with picnic tables and metal-concrete fire pits. An open outdoor amphitheater was built off of B loop, and a fish cleaning house still stands on A loop (although it is used as a maintenance building now). A few years later, almost 100 acres of land was cleared for the lake, and a concrete spillway dam was built to contain the waters of Flatts Creek.

The first swimming area containing a circular man-made island was built on A loop, where today is a volleyball court and canoe launching area. The old stone island is still visible, but overgrown with trees. Until the first portion of Hwy 162/Robbinsville Road/Cherohala Skyway was built, the first campers had to come up the mountain via Rafter Road. Indian Boundary quickly became a favorite spot for locals and tourists alike.

In the late 70's, a new, larger swimming area was constructed with a bath house and restrooms. A tornado wrecked much of B loop in the early 1990's, which closed the old amphitheater.

A quiet moment at Indian Boundary Lake. (*Photo by Stephanie Guy*)

Over the years, the lake and campground have been improved to include a larger swimming area and beach, a concrete handicap-access fishing pier, paved roads, and electricity for RV camping. But overall, the general feel and look of Indian Boundary remains much as it has always been since its construction.

Indian Boundary Lake and its Overflow camping area is accessible year-round, although the developed camping loops and swimming area are limited only for use from April to November.

The First Inhabitants

Humans have lived in and near the Indian Boundary area for thousands of years. Primitive and native peoples did not establish permanent communities in the southeastern mountain areas, but did hunt the wild game prevalent in these areas, as well as traveled the native paths through the area to interact with other distant tribes.

To the native peoples, the mountains were places of mystery, the domain of the bears, mountain lions, and numerous other real and mythical creatures. Even the native peoples had many stories about the mountains that were passed down from generation to generation.

The most well-known native tribes that would have passed through the mountains in the area of Indian Boundary were the Euchee and Cherokee. The nearest villages of these tribes were located along the Little Tennessee River valley from the Citico Creek area to present Vonore, TN, and along the Tellico River from present Tellico Plains to where it joins the Little Tennessee. Almost all of these town sights are now under the waters of Tellico Lake. Tellico Plains takes its name from the Cherokee town of Great Taliquo that was located nearby.

Some of the old mountain paths have been documented and preserved. One such path, known as the Northwest Passage and the Unicoi Turnpike, began near Charleston, SC and continued up through the mountains to Great Taliquo (near present Tellico Plains), passing a few miles south of Indian Boundary through Unicoi Gap.

How did Indian Boundary get its name?

Several "Indian Boundary" lines were set by the British and then the American governments from the 1760's to the early 1800's. British colonial officials set a boundary line that stretched the entire length of the English colonies. The line, running along and near the Blue ridge, was intended to limit white settlement to the east from encroaching on to Indian lands to the west. Over several years, British surveyors marked the line, with a group of Indians there to confirm the correct placement of the boundary. It is the only recorded incident where the English set such a boundary with assistance from the Indians. The intent of the line was good, but it did little to keep out white settlers. Within a few years, the Revolutionary War broke out, and the boundary was no longer enforced at all, allowing white settlers to encroach illegally on Cherokee land.

In 1819, Cherokee leaders negotiated a land sale with the Secretary of State John C. Calhoun, known as the Calhoun Treaty, which sold to the United States all Cherokee lands in Tennessee lying west of the Tennessee River, south of the Little Tennessee River and north of the Hiwassee River. The Cherokee maintained a strip of land north of the Hiwassee that included the historic Hiwassee Old Town, the present corner of the state that is now Bradley and Polk Counties, and the mountainous area that is now the eastern part of Monroe County. This last "Indian Boundary" ran north from the area of present Gee Creek/Hiwassee-Ocoee State Park, northeast through the Whiteoak Flats area where Indian Boundary is now located, as it ran northward to the Little Tennessee.

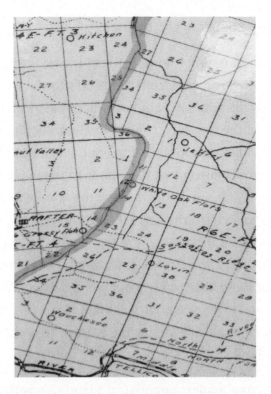

The 1819 "Indian Boundary", separating Cherokee and white settlements, passed directly through the present site of the recreation area. (*Photo by the Author, from a map provided by the Tennessee Trail of Tears Association*)

The last sale of Cherokee land occurred in the Removal Treaty of 1835, which opened all the lands for white settlement. The Cherokee who remained were forcibly removed.

Throughout the 1800's, the area was settled by small mountain farmers who were as rugged and hardy as the land they farmed.

The Civil War brought renegades to the area, who raided and sometimes murdered residents in this no-man's land. In the late 1800's through the early 1900's, the lumber companies came, cutting the timber and laying railroads that would later be used as some of the first actual roads into the area.

The great depression could barely be felt in the mountains, as the mountain people were used to doing without and making their own way. The lumber companies had purchased and ravaged much of the mountain land, and the deforestation left an ugly, gutted, and eroded landscape. The United States Forestry Service eventually bought the old timber lands, as well as many acres of mountain farmland, with the purpose of reforesting and better managing the timber. Many of the mountain people took advantage of the purchase of their lands with the development of the National Forest, and simply moved away. Indian Boundary would eventually be one of the last camping areas built in the National Forest, and with the completion of the Skyway, is a popular tourist destination.

Whether in an RV, camper, or tent, Indian Boundary is a great place to picnic and camp. (*Photo by Stephanie Guy*)

HOW THE SKYWAY CAME TO BE

Sunset on the Skyway. (*Photo by Stephanie Guy*)

Prior to 1996, the journey from Tellico Plains into the nearest towns of Murphy or Robbinsville in Western North Carolina was a difficult one. Trails and rugged "roads" had barely been improved since the 19th century, and except for the old rail beds left by the early 20th century lumber operations, the mountains were barely passible.

And so went the discussion of this situation in a Kiwanis meeting in Tellico Plains in the Spring of 1958. A good, safe road should be built, all agreed, to connect Tellico with its North Carolina neighbors. One of the Kiwanis members, Sam Williams, noted dryly that a better road was needed, "Since our roads are only fit for covered wagons". The other men laughed at first, but then an idea took root: a well-publicized horse-drawn wagon train from Tellico to Murphy, NC, would get public and political attention necessary to fund a new road project.

That July, over 60 wagons and over 300 horseback riders started out on what became the first of an annual wagon train event. For 30 years, the annual wagon train brought more and more attention to the area, and promoted the need for the road.

Views from the Skyway rival any in the country. (*Photo by Stephanie Guy*)

After much surveying and debate, it was decided in 1960 that the road was planned to run from Tellico Plains to Robbinsville. Seven years later, with funding finally secured, construction was begun. In 1996, the road was finally completed and dedicated. Now one of the nation's few National Scenic Byways, the Cherohala Skyway (named for both the Cherokee and Nantahala National Forests through which it passes) offers over 40 miles of some of the most impressive mountain views unobscured by any man-made structure or development, reaching elevations over a mile high as it passes into North Carolina.

The Skyway, also labeled Hwy 143, runs between Hwy 68 in Tellico Plains, TN and Joyce Kilmer Road near Robbinsville, NC. Indian Boundary/Citico Road is 15 miles from Tellico Plains, just two miles off the Skyway.

ATAGAHI, A CHEROKEE LEGEND

Let us begin our storytelling efforts with the Cherokee legend that may explain some of the stranger incidents at Indian Boundary. It is the tale of water, of magic water, that only a few of the Cherokee ever witnessed. It was called Atagahi.

Atagahi (ah-tah-gah'-hee) was known to the Cherokees as "The Lake of the Wounded". According to the legend, animals who were sick or injured could walk deep into the mountains, to a secret cove where lay a sparkling lake. If the animal drank from or touched the magical waters, its wounds or sickness were immediately healed. Only a few Cherokee had ever seen it, and those were only the most skilled hunters with the right spiritual and physical skills who had tracked wounded game to the lake and had witnessed its miraculous powers. But even those hunters were never able to find the lake again, some spending the rest of their lives trying in vain to find it. Even some white hunters, when told of the legend, tried to locate the mystical lake. By the time of the Cherokee Removal in the 1830's, the old Cherokee people simply said that like many other legendary places, Atagahi had become lost, known only to the animals.

Could the waters of Indian Boundary be linked to a Cherokee legend? (*Photo by Stephanie Guy*)

But the belief in healing waters persisted long after the Cherokees were gone. In the late 1800's and early 1900's, several hotels were built in the southeast around mineral springs. One such hotel, White Cliff Springs high atop Starr Mountain, was not far from Indian Boundary. Visitors from all across the country would travel to these springs to drink and to bathe in the waters to heal all sorts of ailments. One hopes the visitors drank the water before they bathed in it!

But Atagahi remains in Cherokee lore. Some say it is lost, others that it simply dried up. Unless, as some believe, Atagahi was located in the shadow of Flatts Mountain, fed by the same waters that now are impounded in Indian Boundary Lake.

The description of Atagahi preserved in "Myths of the Cherokee" by James Mooney is eerily similar to the area of Indian Boundary. Mooney's interviews with old Cherokees indicated that the magical lake was located "westward from the headwaters of the Oconaluftee River (present day Cherokee, NC)", located in a "dry flat" surrounded and containing all kinds of wildlife. And then there are some strange tales of old Monroe County hunters. One old hunter told of shooting a large buck, and tracking it to the edge of Indian Boundary Lake. He at first thought the deer had become dazed and simply swam out into the lake and drowned. But then, to his surprise, he saw the deer leap from the water on the other side, completely healed of the gunshot.

We suppose it is possible that Indian Boundary was built on the same site as Atagahi, that the lake is fed with the same springs that were once revered by the Cherokee, with waters that could heal, or even bring life or extend life. If so, this may explain some other stories...

SOMETHING IN THE WATER: THE DAKWA?

Over the years, there have been several unfortunate drownings in Indian Boundary Lake. While tragedies like this are not uncommon, the nature of at least some of the deaths has been called into question. Some were experienced swimmers. Others were simply wading along the edge of the water. But witnesses say that something seemed to pull some of these unsuspecting victims into the dark water.

Sometimes, during the winter, the lake is drained. And the sight is quite revealing.....and a little creepy. Even after half a century, the stumps of the trees cut to make way for the lake still remain in the lake bottom. Old roads, and a couple of old culvert bridges, weave underneath the waters. Huge ten-foot tractor tires lie submerged, half buried in the lake bottom to reduce erosion. Standing on the fishing pier at the boat ramp, it is clear that one of the deeper and darker parts of the lake is between the pier and the swimming area and around to the dam. Here the lake bottom is marked by a deep trench over 100 feet down. So the dangers of depth and entanglement in half-buried refuse might certainly explain some of the deaths.

The deepest part of Indian Boundary Lake if between the boat ramp pier and the swimming area over to the dam. (*Photo by Stephanie Guy*)

But then there are those who have claimed, from time to time, of bumping into something while they are swimming. And fishermen have told of heavy lines breaking like pieces of string when they were fishing the deeper areas around the dam. Some of these stories bring to mind another Cherokee legend: the Dakwa.

In the 1700's, many white traders along with British and American soldiers passed through the Overhill Cherokee towns along the Little Tennessee River east of present day Vonore. The Cherokee were fond of a story they told about a particular area of the river, near the town of Toqua. There, they would tell, lived the father of the fish tribe, the Dakwa. It was a fish large enough to swallow a man, and was said to have once upset a canoe of warriors and swallowed one of them, at least until the warrior was able to irritate the fish's stomach with a sharp shell and he was able to escape. Another similar story was told of a young boy who, against his father's direction, played too close to the river and was almost swallowed by the Dakwa.

The Little Tennessee River is several miles away from Indian Boundary Lake. So one might initially think there is no way the Dakwa known by the Cherokee could possibly get into Indian Boundary. Except for one thing.....

A closer inspection of Flatts Creek reveals something interesting. After flowing from the Indian Boundary Dam, the creek continues in a northerly course for about 2 miles through the mountains, until finally emptying into Citico Creek, which then flows north and empties into Tellico Lake, which of course is the impounded water of the Little Tennessee River. If a Dakwa, or even a small, young Dakwa fish, hundreds of years ago, were to have swum upstream from its original home near Toqua, then up Citico Creek and then on up Flatts Creek, then it is certainly possible that now, years later, a Dakwa makes its home in the darker, deeper areas of Indian Boundary Lake.

So, we would recommend campers listen to the directions of Forest Service personnel and obey all rules and regulations involving swimming and boating. As long as you stay in the swimming area and wear life jackets when boating, we think you should be OK. Just avoid swimming in the middle of the lake or around the dam. The Dakwa might be hungry.

Flatts Creek as it leaves the dam at Indian Boundary Lake. The waters flow north to Citico Creek, then to the Little Tennessee River/Tellico Lake. Could a large fish from a Cherokee legend swam upstream and be living in the waters of the lake? (*Photo by Stephanie Guy*)

THE HERMIT OF FLATTS CREEK

As white settlers first came into East Tennessee and Western North Carolina, the first lands to be settled were the well-watered valley. The mountain land was settled later, mostly by poor people who could not afford good bottom land. Many were German, most were Scotch-Irish, and they worked their way back into the deep mountains to find a life for themselves. For almost 200 years, the descendants of these people lived almost completely isolated from the rest of society. In the early part of the 20th Century, author Horace Kephart discovered people living along the Tennessee/North Carolina border with much of the same ways and customs their ancestors had, as if they had been caught in time and never changed.

Another story told at Indian Boundary is about a man who once lived where the lake was later built. He was an old mountain hermit who eked out a meager living on a little ramshackle farm in the valley fed by Donnelly and Flatts Creeks. No one knows for sure what his name was, but one name that is mentioned is Falkirk, and so for the purpose of this story that is what we will call him. He was so old, that the few people who knew of him claimed that Falkirk had lived in the flats as long as anyone could remember, and some could only ever recall him as being an old man.

Like many Appalachian people, Falkirk was very independent and distrustful of the government and of the men in its employ. Old Mr. Falkirk also made moonshine, so he was even less inclined to think anything of the government or government men. A story goes that when Indian Boundary was first being planned and the wilderness was being surveyed in the late 1950's, the survey crew happened upon the rickety house and barn of the Falkirk place, so far back on Flatts Creek that few had even known it was there. Old Mr. Falkirk was none too pleased to learn that the government planned to build a dam and flood his home and farm, and refused the men's promise that the government would buy his land at a good price.

 "Thar ain't to price to my land," growled Old Falkirk, dressed in ragged overalls and pointing an old rusted shotgun at the men. "You git off my land and don't you never come back." The men understood the determination in Old Falkirk's grey eyes, and took their equipment and fled.

As the project proceeded, more Forest Service personnel made their way up Flatts Creek, and soon there were more encounters with Old Falkirk. Again, he threatened the men who planned to build the dam, and made a strange statement: "You won't ever get me outna here. I don't keer how many men you send, nor how deep the waters over my head. I'll hook my toes in the mud and stay here fer-ever," he said with a toothless sneer, wiggling the toes of his dirty bare feet, his toenails as long as a bear's claws.

As the project went along, a check was drafted and sent to pay Old Falkirk for his land, but the men who brought it found the

Falkirk house abandoned. Thinking the old man had finally given up, they tore up the check and started cutting trees and building the dam. But soon, the workers reported finding their equipment and trucks vandalized. Bare footprints were often found.

Falkirk was suspected, but no one ever saw anything. Workers cut the spruce and firs of the flats, clearing the way for the coming lake, and eventually worked their way back to the Falkirk homesite. It was in one of the lower parts of the flats, and would be at the bottom of one of the deepest parts of the lake. They tore down the barn, but angry at having so much of their equipment vandalized, they left the old house standing.

"The water will take care of that old, nasty place," said the work crew foremen. But his men were uneasy. They told later that the whole time they were on Falkirk's land, they felt eyes on them. Another worker, speaking many years later, said that when the dam was closed and the water began to rise, he and another man took a boat out to inspect the level of the lake. Just before the waters closed over the Falkirk house, he claimed he saw something moving in the windows. But the waters quickly covered the little shack, and it disappeared forever.

Over the many years, campers and hikers have enjoyed the recreation of the lake. Swimming, canoeing, fishing, and hiking the lake trail have always been part of experiencing the fun of Indian Boundary. But every now and then, a camper returns with an odd sighting.

Sometimes it's a fisherman, who hooks something from his canoe that cannot be reeled in without breaking the line.

Sometimes it's someone enjoying the swimming area. They will claim that they saw something bob up out of the water, far out in the lake. At first, they say, it looks like a soft shell turtle. But the shape is too rounded. Sometimes they even think it is just a swimmer who has swam too far out. Then it disappears.

Photo supposedly taken by a terrified woman of what appears to be a man-like creature, covered in lake moss and slime, swimming away from the edge of the lake. (*Author's Collection*)

Sometimes it's a hiker, who while on the more remote parts of the trail say they have seen the form of a man out in the water, walking around in the lake. One terrified woman claimed to have seen the man close up, surprising him on the trail near the lake's backwaters. She said he was an old man, his skin a pale-green color, dressed in rotted overalls, and no shoes. His eyes were grey, and under his cheeks were what she best described as gills. She said the old man hissed at her, and in a gurgled voice screamed "I'll not never leave hyere!" before he dove into the water and disappeared.

If this story is true, it's another reason to stay within the bounds of the swimming area, and to always wear a lifejacket when in a boat on the lake.

DEAD MAN'S RUN

A few miles past the Tennessee-North Carolina line, in Graham County on the Cherohala Skyway, are a series of "balds", high mountain tops covered only in grass with only a few trees. Hiking trails are maintained to these balds, on both sides of the highway: to the south is Hooper Bald, to the north are Oak Knob and Huckleberry Bald.

Hooper's Bald

Hooper's Bald is named after a doctor from the Robbinsville area who grazed his herds of cattle on the thick mountain grasses. But Hooper was likely not the first white man on the bald. A curious rock on the bald's east side is covered in numerous carvings. One carving, on the lower right of the rock, appears to be in Spanish, reading "PREDARMS CASADA 1615".

It is believed by some that this may have been done by remnants or descendants of men from Hernando Desoto's expedition through the southeast in 1540, who may have left the main group in search of gold and wound up living in the mountains away from the Indians.

In the early 20th century, a group of northern businessmen built and operated a hunting lodge on Hooper's Bald, and shipped in wild Russian boar, bear, elk, buffalo, wild turkey, and other animals. But the bears climbed the fences and the wild hogs escaped under them, and the other animals failed to prosper. The lodge soon fell into private ownership, and eventually burned. The wild pigs that now inhabit East Tennessee and Western North Carolina are descended from the Russian boars who escaped. Today a developed trail takes you on a little over half-mile hike to Hooper's Bald.

This exposed rock on Hooper Bald has carvings that date from 1615. (*Photo by Stephanie Guy*)

Huckleberry Knob

The hike to Huckleberry is short, only a little over a mile, with breathtaking views all around you. But you will also see a grave. It is just off the side of the bald, a skinny, weathered cross over an old gravestone. A plaque placed there in 1999 tells the story of the man buried there, and from this is where we take our next story......

In the late 1800's, the Tellico Mountains were being logged heavily for the huge chestnuts and other hardwoods that had grown there for centuries. In late 1899, the Heyser Lumber Company was operating a logging camp at the mouth of Sycamore Creek where it flows into the Tellico River, near the present location of the Tellico Fish Rearing Pools. And among the workers of that camp were two men from Pennsylvania: Andy Sherman and Paul O'Neil.

It was almost Christmas, and several of the men were planning to go back off the mountains to Tellico to spend the holiday. But Sherman and O'Neil decided they would go across the western mountains into North Carolina, and enjoy the saloons and good times in the rowdy mountain town of Robbinsville. On December 11, they packed a few clothes, some food, and several bottles of whiskey and set out on the trail, up Sycamore Creek, up toward the high mountain passes.

By nightfall, the men who remained in the camp noted that the temperature began to drop. A thick snow began to fall, and to make things worse, a heavy bone-chilling fog moved in. For several days the weather remained so. Eventually, warmer temperatures allowed others to leave the camp for a short break from the work to celebrate Christmas.

After the New Year, men began to drift back to their lumber-cutting jobs at the Heyser camp. But Andy Sherman and Paul O'Neil never returned. It was thought at the time that they had enjoyed too much fun over in Robbinsville, and perhaps had become distracted by the warmth of too many North Carolina girls to make them want to come back to the mountains. As the work continued into the Spring, the two former workers were mostly forgotten.

That was, until the following September. A group of hunters, searching for game under the slopes of Huckleberry Knob, were walking along a stream when they came upon a ghastly sight. Two bodies, reduced mostly to skeletons, lay alongside the creek. Some clothing was also nearby, as well as several whiskey bottles. The Sheriff and Coroner from Graham County were contacted and arrived a few days later, and an investigation was made. Based on the location , the bodies, and the clothing, it was determined the remains to be Andy Sherman and Paul O'Neil. The Sheriff ruled that the men had likely gotten lost in the winter storm on December 11, consumed too much whiskey, and had frozen to death.

O'Neil's skeleton was released to Robbinsville Doctor Robert J. Orr, who used it as a display in his office. Andy Sherman's bones had been badly damaged by animals. They were collected and carried ¾ of a mile to Huckleberry Knob, where they were buried under a small rock. Years later, a metal cross and plaque were added to tell the story of the unfortunate men. Afterward, the stream where the bodies were found gained a morbid name: Dead Man's Run.

Winter in the mountains can be harsh, and winter storms can and do come quickly and with a vengeance. Some of the higher peaks retain snowfall for much of the winter, and it is not uncommon for the cold fog to drift across the mountains, making even driving a hazardous task.

Andy Sherman's lonely grave on Huckleberry Knob. (*Photo by Stephanie Guy*)

It has been said that, as cars have passed slowly over the foggy Skyway on such winter nights, that the headlights will catch an image along the roadside. They say it looks to be a slim man, dressed in winter clothes and a hat, holding a bottle. Some have said he waves as you pass, his eyes wide, motioning as if he is lost. But drivers who have stopped and tried to offer assistance to the man could suddenly find no trace of him.

It could simply be something created by the fog, swirling in the perpetual wind that races across the ridges. Or could it be Andy Sherman, still lost to eternity, still trying to find his way over the mountains.

How to Get There:

Hooper's Bald and Huckleberry Knob are a short drive east on the Skyway from Indian Boundary. Hooper's Bald trail is accessible from a parking lot on the right and is .6 miles to the bald. Huckleberry Knob, at 5560 feet, it accessible from its trail head about ½ mile further on the left. The trail is 1.25 miles to the top, passing over Oak Knob Bald before reaching Huckleberry. It is the highest point accessible from the Skyway, and is the highest point in the Cheoah Ranger District in the Nantahala National Forest. It's summit offers a breathtaking 360 degree view of Tennessee and North Carolina.

THE RANGER

Vintage Ranger, from an old postcard.

Some ghosts are not scary at all. Some are, well, downright nice and helpful.

The lake and campsites are officially known as Indian Boundary Recreation Area. It is part of the Cherokee National Forest, and of course is managed by US Forestry personnel. Volunteer "campground hosts" have for many years also been important parts of the management of Indian Boundary. The hosts, along with the US Forestry Service Rangers, maintenance personnel, and volunteers have worked diligently to keep Indian Boundary safe, clean, and enjoyable for generations of campers.

Does the ghost of a former Ranger haunt the camping loops of Indian Boundary? (*photo by Gillian Roberts*)

Part of the area Rangers duties is to patrol the campground. Sometimes campers get a little loud, to the point they disturb their neighbors camped nearby. Others just don't keep their camp or picnic site clean and trash-free. And others forget to secure food away from the occasional curious bear who might stroll off of Flatts Mountain for a quick snack. And more than one camper has felt the sigh of relief to meet a Ranger's flashlight along a road or trail on a dark, moonless night. Several Rangers have worked their entire careers in the Tellico/Citico areas.

Such was the case with one old friendly Ranger. He loved the mountains, loved his job, and was always extremely helpful to any camper he met. He had been a member of the Civilian Conservation Corps in the 1930's, and had helped build many of the campsites and trails in the area before getting a job with Forestry and becoming a Ranger. He worked his whole life in these mountains, and sadly passed away just days before his retirement.

His friends said it was best that way, that he would never have been happy not working around the campgrounds. His ashes were scattered over the wilderness in a quiet ceremony.

But it seems he was not ready to retire after all.

Every now and then, a camper walking along in the dark has seen a flashlight up ahead, and has come upon an old, friendly ranger. He is known to smile, and is dressed in an old and dated uniform, and sometimes holds an old kerosene lantern. Those who have seen him all agree: he never speaks. If you greet him, he just nods and smiles and goes on his way. Sometimes he's been seen where campers have left trash out, and not kept a clean campsite. Then and only then has he been described as appearing angry, motioning to the mess that needs cleaned up. But if you have become lost, you can ask him to help you find your way, and he is sure to motion for you to follow him. He has never failed to lead the lost camper back to their destination, then, with a smile and a wave, disappears back into the darkness.

DEATH IN WHITEOAK FLATTS

During the Civil War, East Tennessee was deeply divided between Confederates and Union sympathizers. More Union regiments were raised from East Tennessee than any other southern state, which often led to deep resentment between neighbors and kin. As the different armies moved back and forth across the area, allegiances changed, and sometimes men were forced to hide in the mountains until it was their side who was back in control again, or at least until soldiers from the other side rode into town. To make matters worse, bands of bushwhackers roamed the countryside, with little or no allegiances to either side, and taking or killing whatever and whoever they wished.

The Madisonville Democrat Newspaper, publishing some recollections of war survivors in March 1942, printed the account of old Columbus Shaw, who recalled such an incident. Mr. Shaw remembered his mother telling him of 2 Union men stopping and having dinner at the Shaw home, then went across the mountain to hide. But they were murdered in a grisly fashion at Whiteoak Flats, near where Indian Boundary Lake now is.

2 Tennessee Confederates. (*Library of Congress Photo*)

According to legend, the two young men had been away fighting on the Union side, but had gotten tired of the war, and being homesick, had gone AWOL when their patrol had passed close to Madisonville. The two men left their unit, and traveling at night, had made their way to their home in the Mt Vernon area. But they found their home burned, and both parents dead and buried.

With no family left, wanted by the Union Army and considered enemies of the South, the two decided to cross over into North Carolina and start new lives.

But too many people had seen them, and by the time they got their supper at the Shaw home, word of their whereabouts had reached the Kirkland Bushwhackers. This group, led by John Kirkland, were native Monroe Countians and staunch Confederates. Besides this, one of the young men was reputed to have offended a Kirkland girl at a community dance before the war. So as the two men left that night, the Kirklands were spread out in the mountains, waiting.

At some place in Whiteoak Flats, the two men were captured while making camp. They first tried to fight, but the Kirklands were too many. When told to beg for their lives, the men said they'd rather dance with the devil than be obliged to a Kirkland, and so they were killed. One of the more bloodthirsty Kirkland gang members cut the dead men's heads off and set them on fence posts as a warning to any other Union men who might think of passing through. A few years later, their bones were found and buried in a shallow grave.

Legend says the 2 men were killed in the area of present D Loop at Indian Boundary Campground. Campers out walking at night have claimed to have seen two headless men wandering through the nearby woods. Perhaps these spirits are the two unfortunate Union men, fumbling in the darkness where they were murdered so many years ago, still seeking their heads.

THE BIG WHITE DOG

I have heard this story told many times, and one of the places it is connected to is the Tellico Mountains. It is one of the stories that some old campers have heard, and told, around campfires at Indian Boundary.

During the Civil War, many a young man left his mountain home in Monroe County and went off to fight. Few people in the mountains had slaves, and most could see no reason to support the Confederacy. Many of these young men from Eastern Tennessee and Western North Carolina joined the Union army, much to the hatred of their neighbors in the region. One such boy lived in Robbinsville, North Carolina. This young man had from the time of his youth, a large white dog that followed him off to war. Through many camps and a few skirmishes, the dog remained with the soldier boy, and became the company mascot.

When the war was over, the boy and the dog began to make their way home across the mountains. But on top of Flatts Mountain, he was caught by rebel bushwhackers who knew he had served in the Union army and considered him a traitor, and they killed him. The bushwhackers left his body there, and laughed at the dog that refused to leave it. Some other kinder men found the young soldier and buried him, and tried to lead the dog down off the mountain. But every time, the dog would break the rope and go back to his master's grave. Weeks later, the dog was found dead, lying across the grave of the young soldier, forever his faithful friend. It was buried beside the boy, and as time passed the location of the graves were lost.

But as the years went by, stories began to be told of a big white dog that roamed the mountains. Several people claimed to have seen it, even some of the workers who were building Indian Boundary in the mid 1960's. One of the workers was a man we will call Jake.

Jake was a young man from Blount County, fresh out of high school. He had heard about the work at Indian Boundary and though he might get a job there. The problem was, Jake wasn't much of a worker. He was more interested in roadside bars and gambling, and soon proved to be a constant headache for the project foreman for showing up to work half-drunk from the previous night's revelry.

On one such night, Jake had driven down to Tellico for some beer, and by the time he was halfway back up Rafter Road he was "Cooter Brown Drunk". Missing a curve, he ran his old truck into the ditch. He had no choice but to walk back to the work camp at Whiteoak Flats.

Jake later told that he was without even a flashlight, that the full moon came and went behind the night's clouds as he made his way up the road. He had finally gotten to the top of the mountain, just a few miles from the Indian Boundary worksite, when he heard something. Looking over, Jake saw a huge white dog walking along beside him. Still drunk, and in no mood for company, Jake swore at the dog, and yelled "You git on outa hyere!" When he couldn't shoo the dog away, he rared back and gave it a kick. Or at least he tried to. His boot went clear through the white dog.

It was then that Jake realized it was the ghost dog he had heard the other men talk about. He froze. The big dog looked up a Jake with big red eyes, and said:

There, sitting beside him, was the big white dog. It cocked its head sideways, its eyes as red as fire. (*Photo by Stephanie Guy*)

"Are we a-goin home?"

If the sight of the ghost dog had not been enough to terrify Jake, hearing it speak was too much. He screamed and ran for his life, crashing off the roadway into the woods. He tore through the brush and rhododendron, his mind telling himself that he was just drunk and seeing visions. But then he looked over again, and to his horror the big white dog was running along beside him, watching him with its red eyes. And then it spoke again:

"Are we a runnin' home?"

Jake screamed again, and cut off to his right away from the dog. He slipped and fell, and rolled himself up into a heaving ball, trying to catch his breath and his wits. He lay there in the darkness, curled up in the wet leaves, crying and telling himself he was just drunk, that there was no dog chasing him. He lay that way for what seemed like a long time. Finally he willed himself to open his eyes and the moon once more came out from behind a cloud and illuminated the mountainside.

There, sitting beside him, was the big white dog. It cocked its head sideways, its eyes as red as fire.

"We a restin' now, aint we?" it said.

Jake could not stop screaming. He tore to his feet and ran. Now he could see the distant lights of the work camp, and a sprinted toward it yelling for someone to help him. He could hear the heavy feet of the dog in the leaves behind him.

The foreman stumbled from his camper, half asleep, as did the other men of the work crew who were awakened by the screaming. The foreman cursed when he saw Jake running like a madman out of the woods and falling into the camp.

"....that dog!....I ...saw.....right there!......after me!....."

The foreman shone his flashlight into the woods and gave Jake some more cursing. There was nothing there.

"You're drunk again , Jake!" yelled the foreman. "Get in your tent and sleep it off!" Jake's body trembled, and he wiped tears from his eyes as he crawled into his tent. The foreman shook his head and said a few swear words. He glanced out into the woods, and for a minute thought he saw something, something like red eyes. But he shrugged it off, and ordered the other men back to their own beds.

They say that for the rest of the summer, Jake never left the camp worksite, was never late for work, nor drank another beer. In fact, he never drank again.

It is important to abstain from the use of alcohol in the National Forest. Such behavior often leads to late night noise that disturbs other campers, as well as other problems. Persons found in possession of alcoholic beverages in the Cherokee National Forest could face a hefty fine from a ranger or deputy sheriff. Another reason not to possess alcohol in the campground is that it has been rumored that the smell of alcohol and loud noises after hours attracts not only the attention of rangers and law enforcement...but also the glowing red eyes of the big white dog.

JEFFREY'S HELL

Flatts Mountain rises over Indian Boundary Lake directly to the east, giving a picturesque view as it reflects off the waters when observed at the swimming area. It rises up to 3400 feet, and a popular hiking trail across the spine of the mountain gives equally great views of the recreation area and lake below.

But to the east of the mountain, on the other side from Indian Boundary, lies a rugged wilderness area, intersected by numerous mountain streams, the most notable being the north and south forks of Citico Creek. These forks splash through deep, wild valleys to come together to form Citico, about ½ mile south of the road connecting the Indian Boundary area to the Citico and Double Camp area. This confluence is also at the bottom of one of the most well-known and legendary parts of the Citico Wilderness, the area known as Jeffrey's Hell.

Jeffrey's Hell has long held the deepest and darkest secrets in the Southern Cherokee National Forest. *(Photo by Stephanie Guy)*

Jeffrey's Hell is the wildest and most remote part of the Citico area. Its steep mountains lord over deep cuts of thickly-grown vegetation, specifically mountain laurel and rhododendron. Places where mountain laurel grows thick and dense are called "laurel slicks". So tightly interwoven are the twisted branches, these areas are dark, with visibility of only a few feet around you. They are a favorite place for bears and other large animals to hide, and put even the most experienced hunter on his knees, trying to see his way under the laurel branches, in an effort not to be lost in the tangled limbs.

And so it is, how Jeffrey's Hell got its name....

The old mountain people knew the area well, even before it was logged by the Babcock Lumber Company in the 1920's. It has long been told around campfires of the unfortunate hunter, known only as Old Jeffrey, who in the late 1800's, took one last, fateful walk in the area.

The story goes that Jeffrey lived in a remote cabin somewhere in the Citico area. He had no family, and for his living he hunted. What he killed not only fed himself, but he earned a decent wage for the meat he supplied for neighbors and travelers who passed through the mountains.

Jeffrey had prize hunting dogs, likely mountain curs. Having no family, his dogs were like his own children. They lived in his cabin and even ate from his table. The dogs were loyal, obeying every word of their master. They were some of the best tracking, treeing, and bear-fighting dogs around.

One day in late fall, Jeffrey and his dogs went hunting with a party of local men, high up the ridges of Ike's Peak and Brush Mountain, about halfway between Flatts Mountain and the North Carolina line. All day, they trailed deer and bear, and the other men heaped compliments and praises on Jeffrey's dogs. Jeffery, it seems, took a little too much pride in the compliments, and took to boasting about his dogs to the other men. He was so caught up in his bragging, he did not notice as the dogs took off on another game trail, down off the mountain, and into the dark and tangled laurel slicks. When he realized it, Jeffrey tried in vain to call the dogs back, but they were too far gone.

The other men offered words of concern. Everyone knew of dogs and even livestock wandering in to the tangled mess of laurel where the trails became unfindable, places a bear could be on you before you knew it. But Jeffrey would not even look at the other men. He just stared after his dogs.

"I've got to go git my dogs," he said.

The others immediately warned him, reminding him of the dangers of becoming lost in the laurel. "Awwe, Jeff, mebby them dogs of yor'n will find thar way out and back home," they said.

Rugged and choked with rhododendron, the area is named for one unfortunate hunter who went looking for is dogs and never returned. (*Photo by Stephanie Guy*)

But Jeffery was unmoved. "I've got to go git my dogs," he repeated.

"Good lord, Jeffery!" Said one of the men. "That thar laurel is thick as the flames of Hell! You'll not never make it out!"

Old Jeffery turned to face the men, his eyes filled with rage. "I'm a goin' in thar....to git my dogs, or go to hell." And with that, Jeffrey turned down the trail into the setting sun, down the mountain, and into the laurel.

And neither Jeffrey, nor his dogs, were ever seen again.

And so, with the memory of unfortunate Jeffery in their minds, the mountain people called the area "Jeffrey's Hell", both to memorialize the lost hunter, and to warn others who might tempt the deep and darkened wilderness coves, choked with laurel so that even the sunlight could barely get through, and that only a ghost can make it out of.

Perhaps 50 years went by, and the mountain people stayed away from Jeffrey's Hell. Some even said the place was cursed. But in the early 20th century the need for good lumber, and the wealth from its production, began to outweigh old mountain legends. Many mountain families sold their lands to the hungry lumber companies, and soon the sounds of axes and saws drifted over the mountains.

THE JEFFREY'S HELL FIRE

The lumber companies worked their way up the Tellico River first, laying rail road lines up the river as they hauled the giant trees from the virgin forest, some with trunks so large that four men could not join hands around. Stands of oak, poplar, and American chestnut, soon to be wiped out by the great chestnut blight, were felled and either floated down the rivers and creeks or hauled out in loads by the work horse Shay steam engines. But soon the river valley was cut out, and the lines began to snake further up the creek valleys. By the early 20th century, the Babcock Lumber Company had bought out most of the other companies and were pushing its operation back even deeper, going so far as to expand operations and build rail lines from the Little Tennessee River, south, into the Citico area. Lumber camps began to develop as the work progressed farther and deeper into the mountains. By 1925, lumber men were felling trees up the forks of Citico Creek, and even up into Jeffrey's Hell.

The old men who worked the mountain railroad would later tell of that summer of 1925, the "Summer of No Rain". The long, hot summer was a drought, even drying up many of the mountain creeks. And the forests became tinder boxes, so much so that the engineers on the Shay locomotives put screens over their smoke stacks to prevent errant sparks from igniting the dry woods along the tracks. The lumber men and their families in the camps knew that if rain did not come, it was just a matter of time. And every sign of smoke caused people to stop and look, hoping it was not a dreaded forest fire.

That September, crews were working in the mountain coves around a camp called Jeffrey, at the foot of Jeffrey's Hell. The little post office established there had shortened the name to Jeffrey, considering the other word too vulgar for a post office. As crews worked that fateful day, someone noticed smoke far up the ridges, lots of it this time. To their horror, a raging forest fire crested the mountain top and began to race down into the coves, straight for the workers and the people in the lumber camps.

Shay 2147, driven by engineer Fred Presswood, saved over 50 people during a dramatic rescue during the Jeffrey's Hell fire in 1925. It is now on display at the Little River Railroad in Townsend, TN. (*Photo by Stephanie Guy*)

Down Citico Creek sat two Shay train engines with a few flat cars used for hauling logs. One engine, 2147, was operated by engineer Fred Presswood and brakeman Jim Davis. The other, 2890, was piloted by engineer Dave Dockery and fireman Wayne Davis. Knowing they were the only hope for the trapped men and women in the lumber camps, both engineers courageously fired up their trains and chugged up the creek directly into the inferno. Presswood took his engine up the tracks along the North Fork, Dockery took the opposite track up the South Fork.

The railroad split at the "Y" just above the Jeffery Lumber Camp. Presswood took his train left up the North Fork of Citico. Dockery took his to the right up the South Fork. (*Photo by Stephanie Guy*)

The men would later describe it as "the world was on fire". Presswood was lucky. He found several people along the tracks and were able to load up and back out of the fire to safety. But the Dockery train was not so fortunate.

Dockery, too, picked up several people along the track, inching along the steep side of Flatts Mountain. He made it to another lumber camp and was trying to get to a switchback to turn the train around when a giant ball of fire surrounded his train. He'd seen a smoking but already burned off area near where the creek split, and his trainload of about 50 people scrambled toward the possible safety of the clearing as the flames reached his train. But there were two men on board that went the other way, toward the creek: William Graves and Frank Carpenter. Both had been drinking that day, and perhaps it was the whiskey, or maybe the fear of arrest by Deputy Van Cassada who was the area law man and was also on Dockery's rescue train, but the two men headed for the low creek waters.

Dockery's train was trapped on the tracks on the old rail bed to the left. But to the right he saw the clearing across the creek. They made a desperate bid for safety as the flames devoured the train. (*Photo by Stephanie Guy*)

Miraculously, Dockery was able to get the people to the clearing, although his engine caught fire and was quickly destroyed. As the fire passed, the people made their way through the smoke and down the railroad to safety; smoke-clad and singed-haired, but alive. The next day, searchers found the burned bodies of Graves and Carpenter, half covered in the trickle of creek water. Some said the water had gotten so hot it had boiled.

As the fire roared over them, William Graves and Frank Carpenter made the fateful decision to take refuge under a small waterfall in Citico Creek. (*Photo by Stephanie Guy*)

Did the curse of Jeffrey's Hell claim not only poor Jeffrey, but the two lumbermen as well? One can only guess. The mountains are quiet with their secrets.

How to Get There:

The area of the Jeffrey's Hell fire is a short drive and hike north of Indian Boundary toward Citico Creek. Just before the road reaches the creek, park at the trail #105 trailhead. Follow trail 105 as it skirts the west side of Citico Creek. Just upstream, in a small level area, is the site of the Jeffrey Lumber Camp, and here the trail starts to follow the old railroad bed. Some old foundations and chimneys still remain. A little farther, trail #98 bears left at the old "Y", so keep right on 105 up the south fork of Citico. Further up the creek, past the joining of the north and south forks, is the meadow where the 50 people survived the fire. The falls where the two lumbermen perished is also visible just downstream. The area of Jeffery's Hell lies up into the rugged valleys and ridges to the east.

THE MOONSHINER

Indian Boundary now sits on the site of what was once the site of Whiteoak Flats, a remote mountain community of farms that were dispersed over a large, level area with several clear streams. The community included several families and their homes, as well as a school. Almost every trace of this community is long gone, but its stories remain.

One of the houses sat on the hill overlooking the Indian Boundary swimming area, about where the present bath house now sits. The family name is still known in Monroe County, we will just call them the Jones'. As in every community, there is always at least one neighbor who is less than law-abiding. That was Mr. Jones. Mr. Jones made moonshine.

Moonshine, or home-distilled whiskey, has a long history dating back to Scotland and Europe. It was made in many ways, but mostly from the distilled spirits of sugary grains. Europeans found native Americans growing corn, an extremely sugary grain that was well-suited for making alcohol, and from almost the very beginning of the discovery of America, someone was making moonshine.

Many early people considered whiskey an essential part of their diet and used it also as a medicine. But as anti-drinking temperance movements gained momentum, and Prohibition became law, the manufacture, and possession, of moonshine became illegal.

Distillers took their "Stills" into hiding, and the mountains were perfect places to make whiskey in secret. The old folks who recall stories from Whiteoak Flats say that Jones made some of the best.

Jones's still was located somewhere along Flatts Creek, probably below where the lake dam is today. The valley the creek flows through is deep and rugged, with few paths in or out. Jones could take the corn he grew down into the valley behind his house. He could mix it with clear water from Flatts Creek, and let it seep in earthen tubs with some added sugar and yeast until the corn "mash" began to sour. Jones could then sift of the sour "beer" as it was called, and after firing up his still, could make several "runs" distilling the mixture into corn whiskey, hooch, mountain dew, moonshine. At the just the right temperature, after just the right number of runs, Jones could produce whiskey so smooth it would skin you.

Getting rid of his elixir was not too much of a problem for Jones. It was good stuff, and people bought it. He was very careful who he sold to, and was never in much fear of a Federal Revenuer catching him. Having corn whiskey was not Jones's problem. It was that to do with the gold.

Now Jones didn't take gold in payment all the time. Most people around the mountains didn't have any, so he traded whiskey for cattle, pigs, chickens, hay, vegetables, or just about anything he could. He could take wagon loads of these goods and livestock down to the lumber camps or even all the way to Tellico and sell them, and the city people had gold. And as he drove his wagon back up the mountain, Jones did too. And he kept a keen eye out for anyone who might rob him along the way.

Being a mountain-dweller, Jones didn't trust banks. So it was rumored that he made his own banks...out of mason jars. He would fill mason jars with gold coins and bury them somewhere in a narrow cove along Flatts Creek.

Is there a treasure buried somewhere around Indian Boundary? Are there jars of Jones moonshine gold hidden in unknown places, waiting to be found? Maybe, since no one has yet ever found them. It is believed Jones or his family dug up a lot of it as hard times eventually came. The family eventually sold out and moved away, long before the camping area and lake were built.

But the tales are told that maybe he forgot where some of his gold was buried. That maybe it's still out there somewhere around the dam....

Are a moonshiner's gold-filled mason jars still buried somewhere around Indian Boundary's dam? (*photo from Pinterest.com*)

ADVENTURES ON THE LAKE LOOP TRAIL

The Indian Boundary Loop Trail is a 3.2 mile path that circles the Indian Boundary lakeshore. It is accessible from Camping Loop A, from the swimming area, and from the boat ramp. It is graveled, almost entirely level, and for much of its length it is accessible to handicapped hikers, although short parts of the path might be troublesome. But for routine walking, running, and biking, it is a comfortable retreat from the busy campground and swimming areas.

The trail provides close-up views of the lake, and there are several spots that provide access for bank and pier fishing. One of the most exciting parts of the trail is the narrow walk across the dam, with the deepest, darkest water on one side and the spillway flowing into Flatts Creek 100 feet below you on the other. (If you are riding a bike, it's quite a challenge to attempt to ride all the way across without bumping into the safety fence!) The trail passes through pine and hardwood forest, along meadows and under the edge of steep hills. It crosses over several bridges spanning the many small creeks that feed the lake, and it is not uncommon to see wildlife including fish, squirrels, chipmunks, skunks, numerous types of birds, beaver, and sometimes black bear. Whether taking a leisurely stroll or a quick sprint on a bicycle, the lake trail is one of the more popular activities at Indian Boundary.

And, of course, it may be haunted..... or at least inhabited by wild beasts.

Sure, there are the stories: dark images seen in the woods....weird things seen in the water....strange noises in the leaves....crunching gravel behind you, but when you look back, there's no one there.....terrifying things at night, but who in their right mind would walk around the lake at night??!!

I'm not trying to discourage you from experiencing the trail. I've personally been around the lake trail a thousand times, along with my parents, my cousins, old girlfriends, with my wife, with my kids, by myself, in a group, on foot or on a bike. I survived it, and I loved it. I have never camped at Indian Boundary and failed to take at least one tour around the lake trail, and sometimes I've came for just the purpose of a hike, run, or bike ride on the trail. So it's not that I'm issuing a warning. It's more like....an observation....

Let's be honest. As nice as the lake trail is, as peaceful and serene as it may be...it's creepy. There, I said it. It's creepy, and there's no way to get around it. If you don't believe me, take a walk.

You leave the sunny, noisy swimming area and just the short walk to the dam already envelopes you in silence. The dam is a different kind of loud if the lake level is high enough to spill over. Once across, you look back and it seems you're leaving the last vestiges of civilization. Then you walk a little farther and the trail turns back onto the main part of the lake, and you realize you are committed. Soon, it's just you, the trees, the water, and the sound of your footsteps.

The Lakeshore Trail follows a scenic 3.2 mile loop around Indian Boundary Lake. (*Photo by Stephanie Guy*)

Maybe it's the solitude, when it dawns on you that you are way back on the end of the lake, a long way from your car or your camp, and there's nobody around, or at least it doesn't seem like it. Even on a bike, you might find yourself peddling just a little faster as the thought passes through your mind that a mountain lion or bear might just jump out of a tree right on top of you. And then you pass the weird guy, or gal, in shorts that are way too long or way too short; and who smiles at you with a toothy grin, like they are sizing you up in case they decide to eat you. You spend the rest of your walk taking periodic glances behind you, half expecting old shorty-shorts to be stalking you.

And at times, you will be eaten...by bugs. It's Tennessee for crying out loud, and we have summers and early fall that are humid and bug-filled. Mosquitoes, gnats, chiggers, no-seeums, bees, and Satan's own yellow jackets are just a few of the pests that might visit you along the trail. Nothing will make you wish you rode a bicycle more than once a year when you are trying not to run off into the lake after sucking a small, flying insect into your lung.

And do you know what loves a sunny, lakeside trail? Snakes do. And snakes are great pranksters, they are. It must be spoken of with great hilarity in their late-night snake meetings how much they enjoy lying very still alongside the trail until a human comes within about 2 feet and they suddenly squirm and cause what might approach a heart attack and at the least a screaming "Omigosh there's a snake!" dance. Luckily, East Tennessee is only home to two or three venomous snakes who almost never bite anybody. But that doesn't matter much when even the non-venomous ones look like a copper-headed rattle moccasin.

So, if you are of the squeamish type, or have become so after reading this, I might recommend a partner to experience the trail with you. Someone to share in all of its relaxing beauty and occasional frightening wilderness experience, who can provide companionship and support if needed. Somebody with a good eye for snake-spotting, who doesn't forget the bug spray, and whose voice will drown out all the weird forest noises. Someone who might also be alarmed at weird hiker guy, or gal; but who will hang with you and help watch the trail behind you. Someone to distract you if you do happen to get a little spooked. Somebody who can run, but in case of bear or weird hiker attack, not as fast as you can.

But no matter. Take the trail. Get relaxed. Get a little scared. Listen to....nothing. Take in everything. One sure thing about the trail is it is a loop, a circle. Like a good friend, it may give you a lot to think about, but it will bring you back where you need to be.

Numerous wildlife inhabit the Cherokee National Forest, the largest of which is the American Black Bear (Ursus Americanus). Encounters are rare, but can occur. (*photo by Stephanie Guy*)

BIG FEET AND SKUNK APES

The Sasquatch, commonly known as the Bigfoot from the immense tracks it is said to leave, is a mysterious creature reported to have been witnessed predominately in the American Northwest. However, it may surprise most people that there have been reports of Bigfoot in the Eastern United States, even in the Cherokee National Forest. In these areas, the creature is sometimes referred to as the Skunk Ape.

The creatures are described as tall things, covered in shaggy hair, with proportionally large feet and hands, and a face similar to a gorilla but with more human features. There are stories that the Bigfoot has a high level of intellect, and communicates not only be growls and howls, but also by banging sticks and rocks together in a certain pattern, like a primitive Morse Code. Some Bigfoot hunters believe the high intelligence explains why Bigfoot is able to stay hidden from people, through the use of natural camoflage and knowing the most remote routes of travel through the wilderness.

But, they say, Bigfoot is a curious creature as well. Loud noises seem to attract it, as well as food left out in campsites. It is always recommended to keep noise to a minimum and food secured and covered in locations where Bigfoot may have been seen.

The biggest evidence is not the tracks, but the eyewitness accounts of people witnessing the creature's presence. They sometimes are seen standing rigid and still, as if watching humans out of curiosity. Other times they are heard or seen crashing off into the forest when startled. Some accounts say that they are expert swimmers.

There is a website that documents Bigfoot sightings in the Cherokee National Forest, and a frequent contributor to the site says she has had several interactions with the Bigfoot creatures, even to the point as feeding them and giving them names. And yes, there have been supposed sightings of large, hairy creatures around Indian Boundary. Although, these are often found to be hairy, middle-aged men walking without a shirt on.

This photograph was provided to the author by an unidentified source. It appears to have been taken at Indian Boundary. (*From the author's collection*)

Encountering a Bigfoot is similar to encountering a bear. Don't run away, as this sometimes causes the creature's natural instinct to take chase. Rather, wave your arms and make noise. The creature is most likely to take notice of you, then hopefully will move away. Do not leave uncovered food out in camp, as this is an invitation to Bigfoot and bears alike. Both have an excellent sense of smell and will be more likely to come around your camp looking for a tasty snack. Keep all unused food and sugary drinks covered and stored away, preferably in a locked container or inside a vehicle. Also avoid leaving out dirty dishes, stoves, and utensils that may have food on them.

Many campers sometimes report what sounds like something walking through the woods in the camping areas. Other times large trees are found across the lake trail, even when there was no winds the night before. A curious tree can still be found along the trail on the southeast side of the lake, bent in an "s" shape, that some say was the work of a Bigfoot many years ago.

And of course, there are the large tracks sometimes seen in the beach sand in the swimming area. These can sometimes be found in the early morning, before the sunbathers toss towels and toys over the warm, sandy beach. No authentic photos have ever been taken of a Bigfoot at Indian Boundary, so it is wise to keep your camera or phone nearby should you be the lucky camper that can capture one of the creatures on film or video.

SPIVEY COVE

The Tellico Mountains have an immeasurable beauty that brings visitors year after year. The national forest and its rivers, lakes, and streams reflect the images of the towering mountains, and contribute to the large number of campers, hikers, fishermen, hunters, and adventurers who enjoy the area.

The mountains are rugged and remote, and unfortunately these characteristics have sometimes been used by criminals to commit and cover up their crimes, including murder. Within recent memory are several murders either committed along the Tellico River, or bodies hidden in the dark recesses of the mountains.

The story of one such murder stands out in my own memory: in the late 1970's, a local Monroe County man named Joe Shepherd murdered two area girls. One of the murders took place right outside Tellico Plains, just inside the National Forest on Old Furnace Road. Shepherd was arrested after one of the girl's body was found in a shallow grave at his home. But just before his trial, Shepherd escaped jail. For the next ten years, Shepherd was supposedly sighted all over the area, especially in the backwoods. We kids were terrified, thinking this murderer was lurking about in the woods. Every boot print on a mountain trail, every suspicious-looking man, every unsolved crime was attributed to Joe Shepherd. In reality, Shepherd had fled to Canada, and had been living there the whole time until his eventual capture 10 years later. But the stories of "Joe Shepherd" caused us a lot of sleepless nights for the people camping in the Tellico Plains area.

But another story has been long told that makes the hair stand up on your neck. This story is much older than the Shepherd incident, possibly dating all the way back to the 1940's, when the National Forest was created and the campgrounds and recreation areas were built. I have tried to validate this story through newspapers and court records, but I have been unable to do so. It may be that it was lost to history. But I will relate it as it has been told many times to me.

Along the Tellico River, just south of Indian Boundary, lies Spivey Cove Campground. The Spivey Family were pioneer settlers on nearby Spivey Mountain in the early 1800's. The Spivey's moved away in the late 1800's, but the mountain and cove retained the name. In the 1930's a Civilian Conservation Corp (CCC) Camps was established there, and much of the roads and campgrounds construction in the National Forest was done by the men who worked there.

The camp and its building were later dismantled and the campground developed in its place, but a few foundation stones and photographs of the old CCC camp remain.

As the story goes, not long after the campground was built, a young couple drove over the mountains from North Carolina to camp. It was early in the Spring, and no other campers were in the Cove. The camping trip was not one of much enjoyment for the couple: the wife had recently been caught cheating on her husband, and they had decided to go camping to talk things over, and hopefully save their marriage.

Remains if the stone foundation of a CCC Camp building in Spivey Cove campground on the Tellico River. (*Photo by Stephanie Guy*)

The couple drove to the very back of the campground and decided to camp in the last, secluded spot beside the bubbling waters of Spivey Branch. They set up their camper, and as it grew dark they cooked supper and sat beside the fire, trying to talk through the problems of their shattered marriage.

But soon the talk turned as dark as the night. The wife would not reconcile, and told the husband she no longer loved him, and wanted out. In fact, she would pack up her things in the morning, and go directly to a lawyer's office back home and file for divorce. The husband grew angry, having gone to all the trouble to plan the camping trip, and was disappointed in his wife for having ruined their marriage. It was decided that the wife would not share his bed in the camper that night: she took her sleeping bag and spread her a bed on the picnic table. The husband went to his bed in the camper.

As he lay there, his anger grew. She had torn out his heart, and she was ruining his life, his happiness, their future, everything. In a passionate fury, the husband got out of his bed, and walked outside in the darkness. The fire had burned down, but he could see her sleeping form on the picnic table. For a long time, he just stared at her, sleeping peacefully while his whole world crumbled around him. Blinded by his fury, he took up the camp axe. In moments his wife lay a dead and bloodied heap on the table.

Immediately, he was shocked at what he had done. He looked at her mangled body, blood dripping off the table and pooling on the graveled campsite. In a panic, he looked around for some way to hide his crime. They were all alone in the campground. No one had seen it happen. If he could hide her body it might be months before she was found, and by then he would be long gone.

Finding his flashlight, he quickly looked for a place to hide the body. In the creek bed? Perhaps a shallow grave in the edge of the forest? Then he saw the tree.

Beside their campsite stood an ancient, hollow maple tree. About 8 feet off the ground was a huge opening in the trunk. Yes, just large enough to stuff her corpse inside. Rolling up the sleeping bag around her lifeless body, he carried her over and, although it was difficult, was able to slide the dead body of his wife into the hollow tree trunk. Quickly, he took up a large pot and carried water from the creek and washed away the blood that stained the tree, as well as the picnic table and the gravel around the campsite. It took well over an hour to clean up the evidence of his horrible crime, and he stood there in the darkness with his flashlight, looking over the camp one last time. Confident he had covered up the murder, he went back inside the camper and fell into the bed, exhausted from the ordeal.

He awoke with a start, covered in sweat, freezing in the cool mountain air. It was still pitch black dark. What had woke him? Had he heard something? Yes, he thought. Some noise, outside. He got out of bed and grabbed the flashlight. As he opened the camper door the light's beam lit up the campsite.

The back campsite of Spivey Cove has long been associated with a story of murder, told for years around local campfires. (*Photo by Stephanie Guy*)

His heart stopped in his chest.

Blood covered the picnic table, running in little rivulets down on to the gravel where it congealed in little black pools. It also ran down the front of the tree where he'd put his wife's body. Had he not cleaned it all up? No, he must not have, he thought. Maybe in the excitement of the murder, he had simply missed some of the blood. He stepped out of the camper, took the pot, and once again washed away the blood from the picnic table, from the gravel, and off of the tree. He looked down inside the tree to ensure the bloody sleeping bag and its morbid contents were still inside. And once more he stood looking over the campsite with the flashlight, checking everything again to make sure there was no blood, no evidence of the murder he had committed. It was well into the early morning hours, and he was even more exhausted as he went back into the camper. He would try to get some sleep and leave at first light. He was planning ways to empty his bank accounts and head to Mexico when he fell asleep.

Again, there was a noise. He shot straight up from a deep sleep, and sat still for a moment to see if he heard it again. He was so sleepy, he could not say exactly what he had heard. But there was something. Angry, he took the flashlight once more and stepped out of the camper, and once more into a nightmare.

All around the campsite, blood was pooled in the gravel. It covered the table as it had when he had murdered his wife, and again it was on the tree below the hollow place. He could barely breathe. He knew he had cleaned it all up. Once. Twice. Hadn't he? Or had he dreamed it? It didn't matter, he thought. He would make sure this time. He took the pot and carried water over and over again to wash away the blood from the gravel, from the picnic table, and from the tree. Even after it was gone, he carried more water, so much that he forgot how many times he filled the pot. Finally, he was convinced he had covered it up. All evidence was gone, washed away. He checked her body once more. It would not be long until dawn, and it was now the darkest time of night. Clouds passed in front of the full moon as he closed the door of the camper and fell into the bed. He was just tired and his mind was playing tricks on him. When morning comes, I will leave and never come back........never come back.....

The sound this time was unmistakable. He felt like he had just fallen asleep when he heard it, the rustling, crunching sound. He lay there in the blackness, trying to catch his breath. Someone must be outside, he thought. Someone knows what I did. Well they won't know for long. He forced himself out of the bed, and with the camp axe in one hand he pushed open the camper door. He held up the flashlight, and clicked it on.

The blood was everywhere. On the graveled ground, pooled and dripping from the picnic table. The beam from the light followed the bloody trail from the picnic table, across the ground, and up the hollow tree.

He could not scream when he saw her. Her head protruded from the gaping hole, her face half covered by the bloody sleeping bag. It was her eyes that froze him, wide and piercing into his soul. Her mouth opened, and he dropped the flashlight as she laughed with an evil, screeching scream.

(A tip for telling this story: turn out all other lights except your flashlight, which you turn off every time the husband goes to bed. Every time he hears the noise, turn on the flashlight and shine it as if you are the husband seeing the ground, the table, and the tree.

Having a large tree nearby is great. At the end of the story, as you describe the dead wife, as soon as you say the part about her laughing scream, shine the light slowly up the tree trunk, and after about 2 seconds of silence, laugh with a screeching, screaming laugh. It gets them every time!)

Beware of the hollow tree.
(Photo by Stephanie Guy)

CAMPING TIPS

When it comes to what not to do on camping trips, I've seen it all. Everything from unorganized campsites, rude and inconsiderate campers, animals invading to get to unattended food, drunken fights, loud music, swarms of skunks, storm-flooded tents, to tripping over equipment in the dark. (I must admit I have, in the past, sometimes been guilty of some of these mistakes myself).

So to hopefully help you avoid the mistakes of others, here are a few tips and suggestions on how to have an enjoyable, hassle-free, and injury-free trip to Indian Boundary.

<u>Keeping a Clean and Quiet Campsite:</u>

Keep all trash picked up, burned, or bagged.

Keep all camp equipment stowed away when not in use.

Keep all food covered and secured in a locked container or inside a vehicle if unattended. This is a requirement in the National Forest.

Keep noise to a minimum. Try not to disturb other campers. If you are a night-owl who likes to sing songs around the late-night fire, try to pick a campsite away from others who value their uninterrupted sleep.

It is important to keep your campsite clean. Not doing so invites wild animals into camping areas, can cause injury and trip hazards, and overall is unsanitary. (*Photo by Stephanie Guy*)

Prepare for Rain and Storms

Rain and thunderstorms can ruin a good camping trip. Being wet is uncomfortable, cold, and can lead to hypothermia even on a warm night. Always keep this in mind where you pitch your tent or set your camper.

When choosing a campsite, look for natural drainage. If rain is in the forecast, avoid campsites that are on low ground where rainwater could flow into your camp, or has a "dry creek" that might flood or overflow in a bad rainstorm. Watch for dead trees and limbs that could fall or be blown into your campsite by high winds.

Stay on the Roads and Trails

Nothing would ruin a good camping trip worse than getting lost. At best, being lost is scary, uncomfortable, and embarrassing. Indian Boundary has a pleasant and easy three-mile trail around the lake that is popular with campers for walking, running, or biking.

It is important to first let someone know before you go for a walk, and where you intend to go. That way, in case you are lost or injured, someone at least knows where to start looking for you.

Second, stay on the developed and marked trails, to ensure that you are able to make it back to camp. It is wise to be taking a small amount of food and water with you on even a short hike.

If you do make the mistake of going off on your own and getting, as Daniel Boone once said, "A might bewildered", If you realize you are lost, stay in one place, make noise, and listen for others who may be searching for you.

For safety sake, always stay on marked trails. (*Photo by Stephanie Guy*)

Swim ONLY in the Designated Swimming Area

Few, if any, drownings or swimming accidents have occurred within the designated swimming area. It is important, nay, life-dependent, to stay within the markers and out of the deeper areas of Indian Boundary Lake. The lake is beautiful, but also contains numerous natural hazards besides depth, including wildlife, trees and other underwater hazards.

Swimming only in the swimming area alleviates almost all concern for these dangers.

Use a Life-Jacket

It should be common sense to wear a Personal Flotation Device (PFD/life jacket) any time you are on any body of water. Boating or canoeing Indian Boundary Lake is no different. Having lost close friends to drowning when a simple life vest would have saved their life, I personally stress this to my own family and fellow outdoors enthusiasts. Don't be a statistic: wear a PFD, or stay out of the boat.

Building a Camp Fire:

A campfire is a central part of the camping experience. For thousands of years, people have sat by campfires and cooked, talked, told stories, planned battles, warmed themselves, and sometimes simply enjoyed the fire. Have you ever camped alone? A camp fire can also be a companion on a dark, lonely night. Henry David Thoreau, in his book "Walden", says: "You always see a face in the fire".

But building and maintaining a fire also requires care and responsibility. You want your camping experience to be full of great memories, not burns and damaged property.

First, assemble your tools. You will need:

1. Dry firewood. At Indian Boundary, firewood can be purchased at the camp store. Note that there are requirements for bringing in firewood into the National Forest, as well as regulations for picking up downed wood. Be familiar with these rules and laws, and if you have

questions, ask a campground host or Forest Service Employee. Also avoid using loud saws as this is not pleasant to other campers.

2. Dry kindling, smaller pieces of wood. The same rules apply as mentioned above.

3. A Firestarter. This could be rolled up newspapers, recycled toilet paper tubes filled with dryer lint, or even store-bought fire starters. These starters are intended to catch the flame from your ignition source and provide a slow, steady flame to catch your kindling.

4. Ignition source: unless you are making a primitive fire, this is normally matches or a lighter.

5. A clear, dry fire pit. Indian Boundary requires your fire be maintained within the fire pit provided with your campsite.

6. CAUTION: the use of accelerants such as fuels, or highly flammable items are not recommended, as these can cause flashfires, burns, and explosions.

7. If the area is experiencing drought conditions, make sure it is legal to even build a fire!

Next, inspect your fire pit:

1. Is it dry and clean of trash and other debris? Are all other items moved away to a safe distance?

2. Is the wind blowing? Ensure that no part of your fire, not even its embers, could blow on to flammable items like the surrounding forest, fabrics, people, etc.

3. Is the fire pit operational? If not, consult with your Campground Host.

Build your fire:

1. Place your fire starter in the fire pit. Place your kindling on top of your fire starter, starting with the smallest, dries pieces first. This can be done either in a criss-cross or a teepee method.

Place tinder or fire starter under a criss-cross or pyramid of small, dry wood. Light and feed more wood slowly. (*Photo by Stephanie Guy*)

2. Use your match or lighter to light the edges of your fire starter. As your kindling begins to catch, add small pieces of fire wood. Do this slowly, like you are feeding a small child. Slowly feed the fire small, then larger, pieces of wood as it slowly begins to "eat". Don't rush it.

Slowly add larger dry wood to your fire, Build in a slow, methodical manner. (*Photo by Stephanie Guy*)

3. CAUTION: don't build your fire too big, just big enough to be warm enough to comfortably sit by and provide enough light for the surrounding area and to cook on. A small fire is always best, as it is easy to manage, doesn't use too much wood, and can be put out quickly if necessary.

Maintaining your fire:

1. Add wood only as necessary to keep your fire comfortable.
2. NEVER leave a campfire unattended.
3. Avoid alcoholic beverages. Yes, drunk people will fall into a fire.
4. Keep children at a safe distance.
5. Keep a container of water close by to extinguish the fire if necessary.

Keep your campfire just large enough to provide the right amount of heat for warmth or cooking. (*Photo by Stephanie Guy*)

Now you should have a classic, enjoyable campfire! Prop up a chair, make a "s'more", sing some songs, and tell a good story.

Campfire Legend:

Growing up, I learned from old people a way to keep smoke out of your face as you sit around the fire.

When the smoke gets in your eyes, simply say "I hate rabbits". I know...it sounds silly. But it works! You have to have a little faith in it, and sometimes you have to say it a few times, maybe even a little loud so the smoke can hear you, but it has been proven to work.

Supposedly, this comes from an old Cherokee method. According to an old tale, there was once a fire-spirit that was trying to keep a fire burning, but a group of troublesome rabbits kept trying to put it out. The fire spirit grew to hate the rabbits, and would blow the smoke into their tender eyes to keep them away. If the fire spirit hears "I hate rabbits", it will know you are a friend and move its smoke away from you.

WORDS AND ADVICE FROM EXPERIENCED CAMPERS, RANGERS, AND VOLUNTEERS

<u>Bob Miller, retired Athens City Fire Chief, former Campground Volunteer:</u>

"You could always sit back at Indian Boundary and just enjoy what God has created. It's a very serene place. Having no cell service was always a blessing, but could also be troublesome at times. I always enjoyed meeting people from all over the country who shared my love for the outdoors and camping, and I developed a lot of long-time friends. "

"On the negative side, you always have to watch for snakes and the occasional bear. Severe weather can be a problem if you are not aware and prepared. Sometimes folks built too big a fire and let it get into the woods around camp. Putting up your food to keep it bear-proof is a must. Sometimes people brought vehicles that were too big for the roads and the campsites. And people clogged up the toilets a lot with different stuff. But we only had a few instances of people indulging in too much alcohol and getting to loud or having arguments. And of course, there were the occasional rude campers who though the whole place belonged to them."

Wallace Graham, Retired District Ranger, USFS:

"After working in National Forests in Northern California, Central Louisiana, Arkansas, and Alabama, I was district ranger in Tellico from 1977 to 1989. Indian Boundary fell under my administrative responsibilities."

"Being District Ranger placed me in a head management position, responsible for all employees in the Tellico District. We handled the management of many aspects of the forest, including forestry, watersheds, timber, and recreation."

"One of the challenges we faced back then was implementing the fee system for use of recreation areas. This wasn't something local people and people who had been using the sites supported at first. But after a while, they began to see how important those fees were to continue to operate the areas."

"There were a couple of law enforcement issues that stand out. For a while, we seemed to have a lot of "city" groups who wanted to come to the national forest and have big parties with alcohol and narcotics. But we always had a good relationship with the Monroe County Sheriff's Office and we worked together to shut that down pretty quickly."

"Another incident I recall was a biker gang who came into Indian Boundary and set up camp in the Overflow Area. Me and the county deputy went in there, and the deputy...he was just a fearless kind of guy from the mountains himself....he just walked into the middle of them and said, 'Now, you all are welcome to camp here, but if there are any problems, I'm going to take every one of you to jail'. Well they must have gotten the message because they weren't the least bit of trouble, and when they left that Overflow was cleaner than it had ever been."

Steve Rickerson, retired District Ranger, USFS

"I worked at Indian Boundary from 1980-84, and prior to that I worked in the Ocoee District and afterward at the District Offices, the Cheoah District in North Carolina, and eventually retired as District Ranger working in Alabama. While in the Tellico District, I worked for Wallace Graham as Assistant Ranger."

"Working in the Tellico District was the best assignment of my career, and Wallace was the best boss I ever had. I have some of the fondest memories working that area."

"Back then, we called what is the Skyway today the Robbinsville Road, and construction would start and stop depending on funding and environmental issues. Like one time, some erosion of a specific exposed mineral killed a lot of fish in streams flowing down into North River. We also had programs to employ people 55 and older, as well as the Young Adult Conservation Program that created jobs for younger people. Both programs allowed for a lot of maintenance jobs around Indian Boundary."

"One 4th of July, I remember we had over 1000 people in the campground, and we ran out of water. We took an old fire pump and pumped water from a nearby creek into the holding tank and treated it with chlorine. Thankfully, nobody got sick, but Wallace was pretty concerned when he found out. And for a few years, we would let people shoot off fireworks at the beach on the 4th, but of course we had to stop that."

"I worked with a lot of characters. Bill Cheeks was one. He and I were checking trails in the Slickrock area, east of Citico, one year. We hiked in and spent the night. The hiking in there is hard and steep. When I got home, I found a 20-lb rock that Bill had slipped into my pack! He was probably a little nervous when I sat that rock on my desk when I did his annual performance evaluation a few weeks later."

"Before Wallace, some of the old Rangers were Cap Price and Joe Floyd. Cap got transferred to Tellico after he fired a machine gun over the heads of a rioting crowd in Robbinsville. Joe Floyd worked around the Tellico River even before Indian Boundary was built. He had an old Dodge truck that was constantly tearing up on him. It somehow wound up in the river one day above Bald River Falls, and we suspected Joe had finally had enough of the old truck and let it roll off into the gorge."

"One strange and tragic event I recall was when I was in Cheoah, a young man from Wisconsin came in asking about the trails around Bob Bald. I talked to him for a long time, and gave him some maps and information. But a few days later he was reported missing by his family. We searched for 2 weeks and all we found was his tent near Stratton Meadows. But too long after, 2 guys hiking in Slickrock found a pack, and when I saw it I recognized it was his, and it had his return plane ticket to Wisconsin still inside. We searched there, and eventually found him. He'd fallen off a 30-foot cliff and died, and of course the bears had gotten to his body. He'd wandered far off his course, maybe because of the drugs in his backpack. It was pretty sad. It's always important to tell people exactly where you are going, and to stay on the trails."

"On a happier note, I also remember one Saturday a girl was tubing in the Tellico River and got her foot hung in some rocks. It started to rain and the river was rising. A bunch of us took some plywood and held it up as a makeshift coffer dam to keep the water from covering her. Beecher Colvin took seatbelt straps and worked her foot out. Luckily, it all worked out, and we were able to save her from drowning. There is a plaque at the Tellico Ranger Station honoring everyone who helped."

"My advice to visitors to Indian Boundary is to be courteous, pay your fees, and follow the rules. Be careful of being too loud, most people don't realize how much noise they make."

The author with Mr. Genis Best, 14-year Campground Host and Maintenance Supervisor

Stephanie and I interviewed Genis Best in late March, 2019, at his maintenance area campsite. He had been recommended to me by several old-timers, and was a wealth of information about the Indian Boundary area. He is a kind and personable man that embodies the richness of Indian Boundary.

Genis has personal connections to this area. His grandfather was Jake Best, son of a German immigrant, who in the 1800's settled on Doublecamp Creek in the Citico area, just above Crowder Branch below Farr Gap. Jake farmed and raised cattle and hogs which he herded to markets in Knoxville. He also built a church near his home. When the Forestry Service later built a camping area on Citico Creek on land that Jake had once owned, they named it Jake Best Campground.

"I started camping here many years ago, and liked it. I've always preached some but I retired from construction work, and became a campground host. My last church was Miller's Chapel, which is nearby. The campground host program was the idea of Bill Cheeks and Beecher Colvin. Each loop has its own host, who is there to assist campers with anything they need and to make sure everyone has a good time."

"I love meeting people, and I've met people from all over the United States who've come to Indian Boundary to camp. You get to know people well, and sometimes you even get Christmas cards from them. Sadly, a lot of the campers who were coming when I started have passed away."

"I've seen very few problems at Indian Boundary. Sometimes people might break some rules, like parking in the wrong place or making too much noise. But mostly people treat each other like family. Campers watch out for each other, watch out for the kids who are playing in the loops. That family atmosphere has always been here."

"My advice to campers is enjoy the family atmosphere. Maybe watch out for snakes and yellow jackets. Always remember that our gates close at 10PM, and there is no entrance after that. We can let people out is there is an emergency, but nobody gets back in. And keep food items put away-that's very important."

"As far as experiences, a few stand out. A nice couple camped here several years ago with some little dogs. A skunk came through in the night and the dogs got sprayed. And it was bad. They smelled so bad the couple couldn't put them in the car to leave. Luckily they were pulling a little boat on a trailer, so they put the dogs in the boat and pulled them home."

"We don't have real bad bear problems, but we've had some run-ins. One time, a man came banging on my camper door, hollering "There's a bear in our camp!" So I went over there and see their picnic table is covered in all kinds of food, even chocolate cake, and the bear is sitting at the table, like a person, eating the food. So I ran the bear off and told the guy he might want to put up all the food, but they were all so scared they wouldn't get out of their truck, so I had to clean it all up for them."

"Another time, a guy came running up to a camp host yelling "A bear is in my camp!" The host said, "Well, just bang some pots and pans together and it'll scare him off." The man looked kind of funny and said "I ain't got no pots and pans! Just Tupperware!"

FOR FURTHER READING

I do hope you've enjoyed this book, and I certainly hope it adds to your great experience at Indian Boundary. If you want to read deeper into some of the stories, here are some sources for more reading:

"Atagahi, A Cherokee Legend"; "Something in the Water…the Dakwa?"

- information from these Cherokee legend stories were taken from "Myths of the Cherokee" by James Mooney. The stories are adapted to the area by the author.

"The Hermit of Flatts Creek"; "The Ranger" , "Big Feet and Skunk Apes"

-local stories told at Indian Boundary, by the author.

"Dead Man's Run"

-information for this story comes from the plaque at Andy Sherman Grave; "Roaming the High Country", article by Marshall McClung, grahamcounty.net

"Jeffreys Hell"

-information was taken from area legends, as well as:

"Jeffrey's Hell Inferno of 1925 Recalled", article by Willard Yarbrough. Knoxville News-Sentinel; and article by Rev. CA McKenzie, both reprinted in "History of Monroe County, Tennessee", Vol 1, Part 2, pp 489-491. Sarah G Cox Sands. Gateway Press, 1982.

"A Pictorial History of the Tellico Plains, Tennessee Area (1849-1949)" The Collections of Charles Hall, by Pamela Hall Mathews. Tellico Plains Publishers, 2011.

"Death in Whiteoak Flats" , "The Moonshiner"

-local lore, also based on historical information in the Madisonville Democrat Newspaper, March, 1942

"The Big White Dog"

-this is an old Appalachian story, adapted to Indian Boundary by the author

"Spivey Cove"

- local lore, a ghost story and legend told for many years from numerous sources

While camping at Indian Boundary, appreciate the natural beauty and the history. But don't take life, or campfire stories, too seriously. (*Photo from author's collection*)

Have you made some good memories at Indian Boundary, or heard a good story? Add it here:

ABOUT THE AUTHOR

Joe Guy is an author, outdoorsman, hiker, and storyteller from McMinn County, TN, where he serves as Sheriff and County Historian. He has published several books on local and regional history, including:

Indian Summer: The Siege and Fall of Fort Loudoun

The Hidden History of McMinn County, TN

The Hidden History of East Tennessee

The Hidden History of Southeast Tennessee

A Postcard History of Athens and McMinn County

guyjd@hotmail.com

Joe Guy

Made in the USA
Monee, IL
19 July 2020

36429874R00062